Meditative Coloring Book 2:

CROSSES

Aliyah Schick

Sacred
Imprints

Other Books by Aliyah Schick

- *Mary Magdalene's Words: Two Women's Spiritual Journey,*
  Both Truth and Fiction, Both Ancient and Now.
- *Meditative Coloring Book 1: Angelic Imprints*
- *Meditative Coloring Book 3: Ancient Symbols*
- *Meditative Coloring Book 4: Hearts*
- *Meditative Coloring Book 5: Labyrinths*
- *Finally, a Book of Poetry by Aliyah Schick*

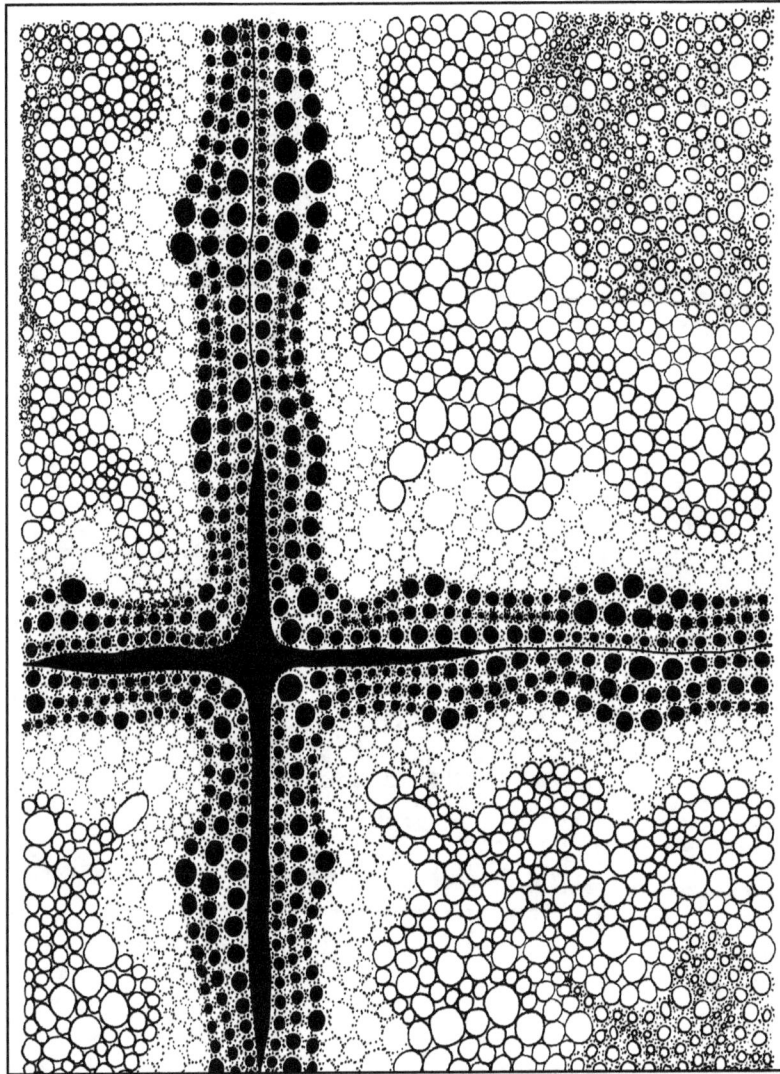

Table of Contents

Dedicated to
peaceful moments,
open hearts,
and
self-discovery.

What Are Sacred Imprints™?

Each of these original pen-and-ink drawings is a unique work of art created through spiritual guidance by artist/healer Aliyah Schick. The drawings of the Crosses Series feature ancient and contemporary images of the cross, reflections of the deep spiritual significance of its form. In the *Crosses Meditative Coloring Book 2* these drawings serve as a chalice for your own meditative communion through the contemplative application of color.

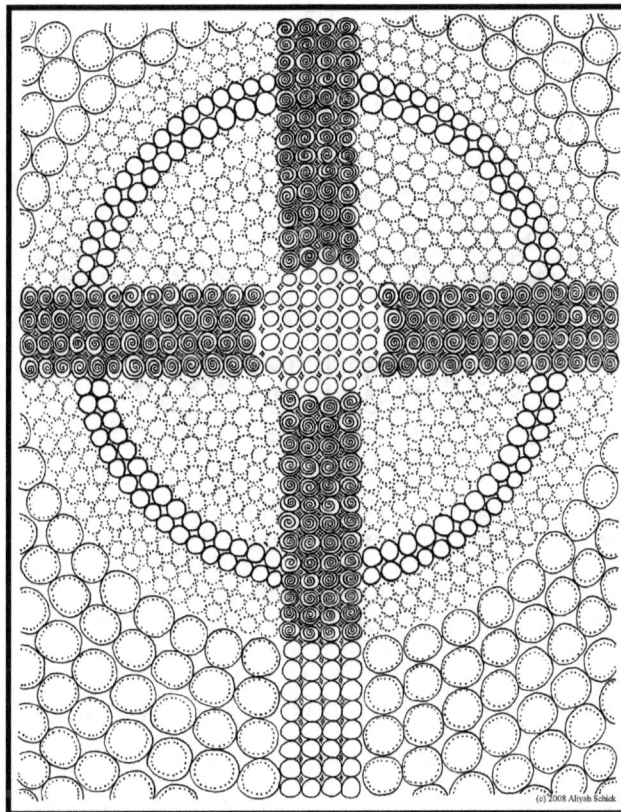

The cross is one of our most ancient and enduring sacred symbols, found in nearly every culture throughout human existence. It symbolizes the celestial, spiritual, divine coming into being in the material world. It represents God taking form, and the integration of soul into full life. At the center of the cross, at that finite point marked by the cross, is the act and moment of coming into being.....creation. This crossing point is the sacred expressing itself in material form, spirit becoming flesh. It is divine mystery manifesting and realizing itself.

(c) 2008 Aliyah Schick

The circled cross is a sacred symbol common to nearly all human existence. What happens when we draw a circle around that point of creation? The circle is a universal symbol, also. It represents wholeness, unmanifested potential, fulfillment, the feminine, cycles, and timelessness. In the circled cross, the circle surrounds and embraces the cross's center. The circle holds that mystical coming together of spirit and matter into manifest being. The circle becomes container for, and participant in, God's expressing and creating all that is.

The cross is both finite and infinite. Its lines mark and hold a single point. Its shape reaches out in all directions. The circle is also both finite and infinite. Its shape encloses and defines a finite space. Its line is never ending. Each of these shapes is paradoxical within itself. And yet they express the same paradox oppositely. In line, the cross defines one point, while the circle's line is infinite. In form, the circle defines and limits, while the cross points to infinity in every direction.

The paradoxes of circle and cross play off each other when they come together, creating a new, more complex level of paradox, paradox upon paradox, multiplying paradoxes. The manifestation of being, the transformation of spirit into form, occurs in this burgeoning paradox and is born of potent, fecund paradoxes, proliferating impossibility, boundless mystery, all beyond our understanding.

Perhaps we need both circle and cross. Perhaps we need both the coming together and the holding, in order to allow and enable that dynamic creativity of spirit's coming into physical form, in order to enable the sacred to come into being, in order to allow the sacred to be.

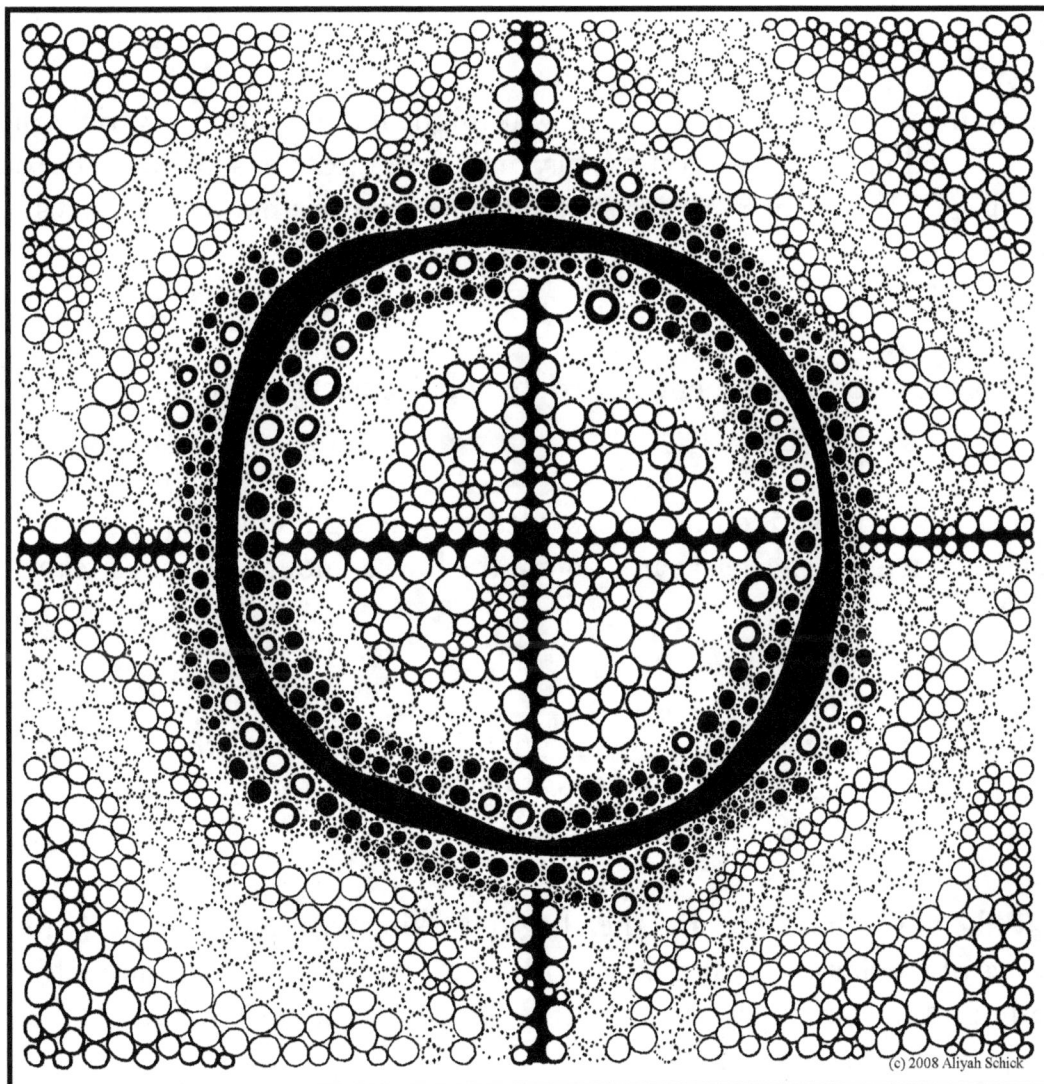

Suggestions for How to Use This Book

Use this *Sacred Imprints*™ *Meditative Coloring Book* for spiritual connection, prayer, relaxation, healing, centering, and for coming into your deep, true self. You may simply wish to experience the images in quiet contemplation. Or, you may focus on a prayer or an affirmation as you work with colors. You may ask for understanding regarding an issue you are dealing with. You may ask for a clearer sense of some aspect of yourself and how it serves you. You may wish to learn about your path or purpose in this lifetime.

Open your heart and your mind as you use this *Sacred Imprints*™ *Meditative Coloring Book*. Pay attention to impressions and ideas, feelings, intuition, and messages. They may very well be exactly what you need to hear.

Tools
Choose your favorite coloring tools, or you might like to gather a variety of pens, crayons, colored pencils, chalk, oil pastels, markers, glitter pens, paints, etc. You may want to place a blank sheet of paper behind the page so ink or paint does not go through.

Music
Consider playing soft instrumental or contemplative background music.

Nature
Sometimes a favorite spot outdoors provides just the right environment for creative expression. Beach, woods, backyard, porch, treehouse, mountain top, stream, pond, park, etc.

Silence
You may prefer quiet, so that all your attention focuses on what you are doing. Emptiness can give rise to profound experience.

Meditation
You may like to meditate first, and then begin working with the colors. Try any of the many ways of meditation, or simply be with your breath for a few minutes, following it in and out. Or, you may wish to try the following meditation. Read it silently or out loud, slowly, pausing to draw in each breath.

Meditation

Take in a breath… and on the exhale release the day's happenings, settling into this peaceful time of creative, spiritual connection.

Take in a breath… and on the exhale let go of worries and troubles and burdens. You can pick them up again later if you need to.

Take in a breath… and on the exhale come into the center of your Self. From there drop a line down through your body, through the chair and the floor and into the earth. Through soil and sand and stone, through coal and underground stream, and minerals and precious metals. Down through all the colors and textures and densities of the earth, down into the hot magma at this planet's core. Down to the very center of the earth, to the Heart of the Mother. Tie your line there. Anchor yourself there.

Take in a breath… and on the exhale extend your line up from your center, through your body and out the crown of your head, up through the ceiling, through the roof, and into the sky. Past clouds and wind and thinning gases, out through the atmosphere and into space. Past the sun and galaxy and stars and universe, out to the depths of the Source of All That Is. Feel your connection there. You are part of the great cosmos. You are one with all being.

Take in a breath… and on the exhale return to the drawing before you and ask that you be open to receiving guidance and understanding as you spend time with it. Know that there are no mistakes, only new choices and combinations and patterns that suggest new perception at an other-than-conscious level. Or that remind us of something that can now be released. Or that create an opening to new possibilities.

Take in a breath… and on the exhale release "shoulds" and rules and expectations. Let go and open to new possibilities.

Now, begin by picking up whatever color catches your attention.

About the Artist

Aliyah Schick has been an artist all of her life. After Peace Corps in the Andes Mountains of South America, she studied art full time for four years, then created and sold pottery and ceramic art pieces for many years. Later Aliyah worked in fiber and fabric, making soft sculptural wall pieces and art quilts, then fabric dolls designed to carry healing energy. Now she draws and paints, and she writes poems and prose.

At the heart of all this, Aliyah's real work is healing. She is a skilled and dynamic deep energetic healer. Her work in the multidimensional layers and patterns of the auric field is powerful and effective. The *Sacred Imprints*™ and the *Meditative Coloring*™ *Books* emerged as new expressions of Aliyah's healing work. Experiencing these drawings serves to remind us who we are, where we come from, and why we are here.

Aliyah lives and works in the beautiful Blue Ridge Mountains of North Carolina, where the energy of the earth is easily accessible, ancient, motherly, and obvious. A place where people speak with familiarity and reverence of the land and spirit, and where the sacred comes to sit with us on the porch to share the afternoon sun.

www.AliyahSchick.com

The
Drawings

Opposite each drawing is a blank page labeled Meditative Impressions. Use these pages to catch and keep hold of your thoughts, wishes, intentions, affirmations, prayers, poems, memories, notes, drawings, or whatever comes to you as you explore coloring with this book. Make it yours.

11

13

15

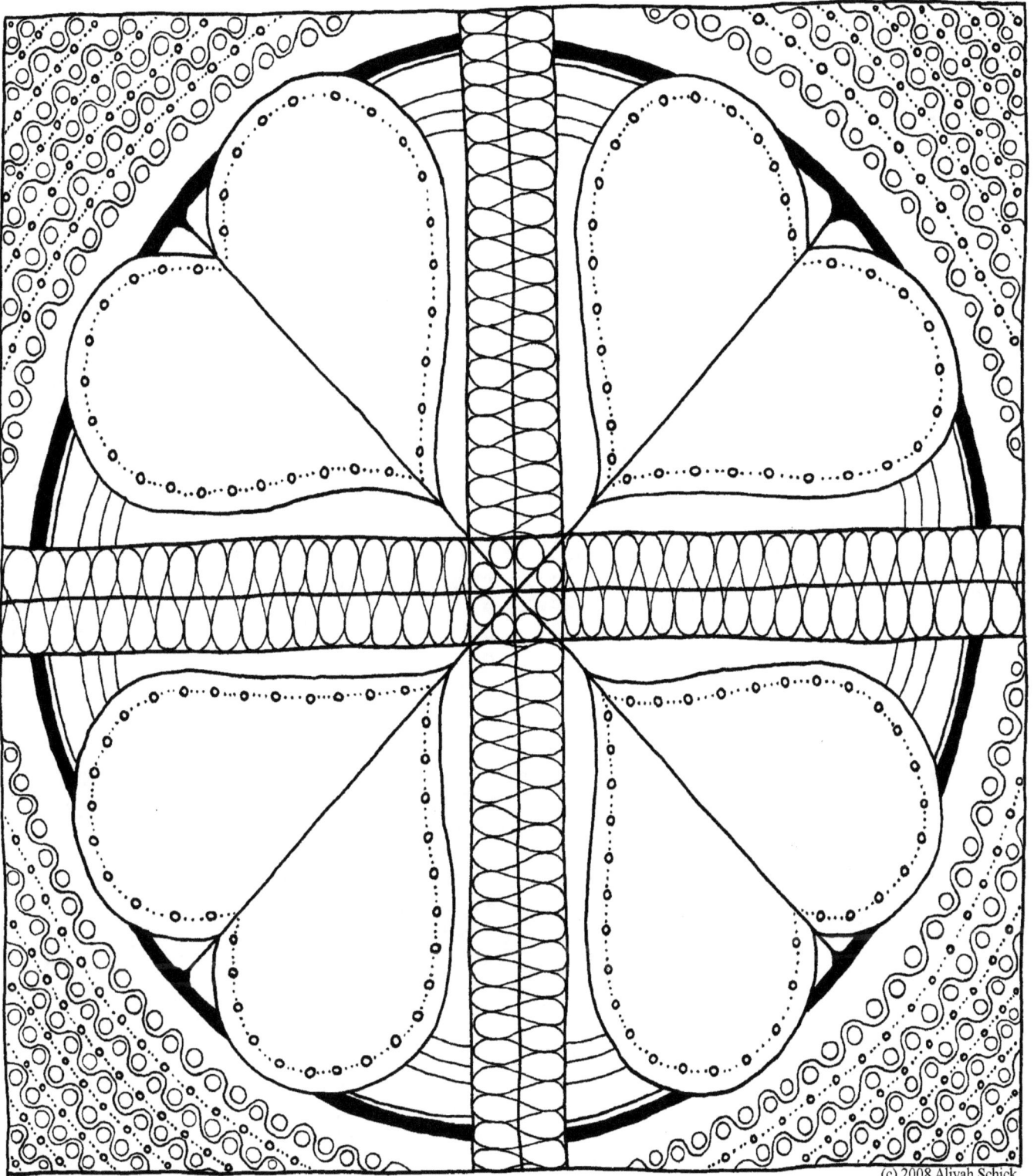

17

19

21

23

25

27

29

Meditative Impressions

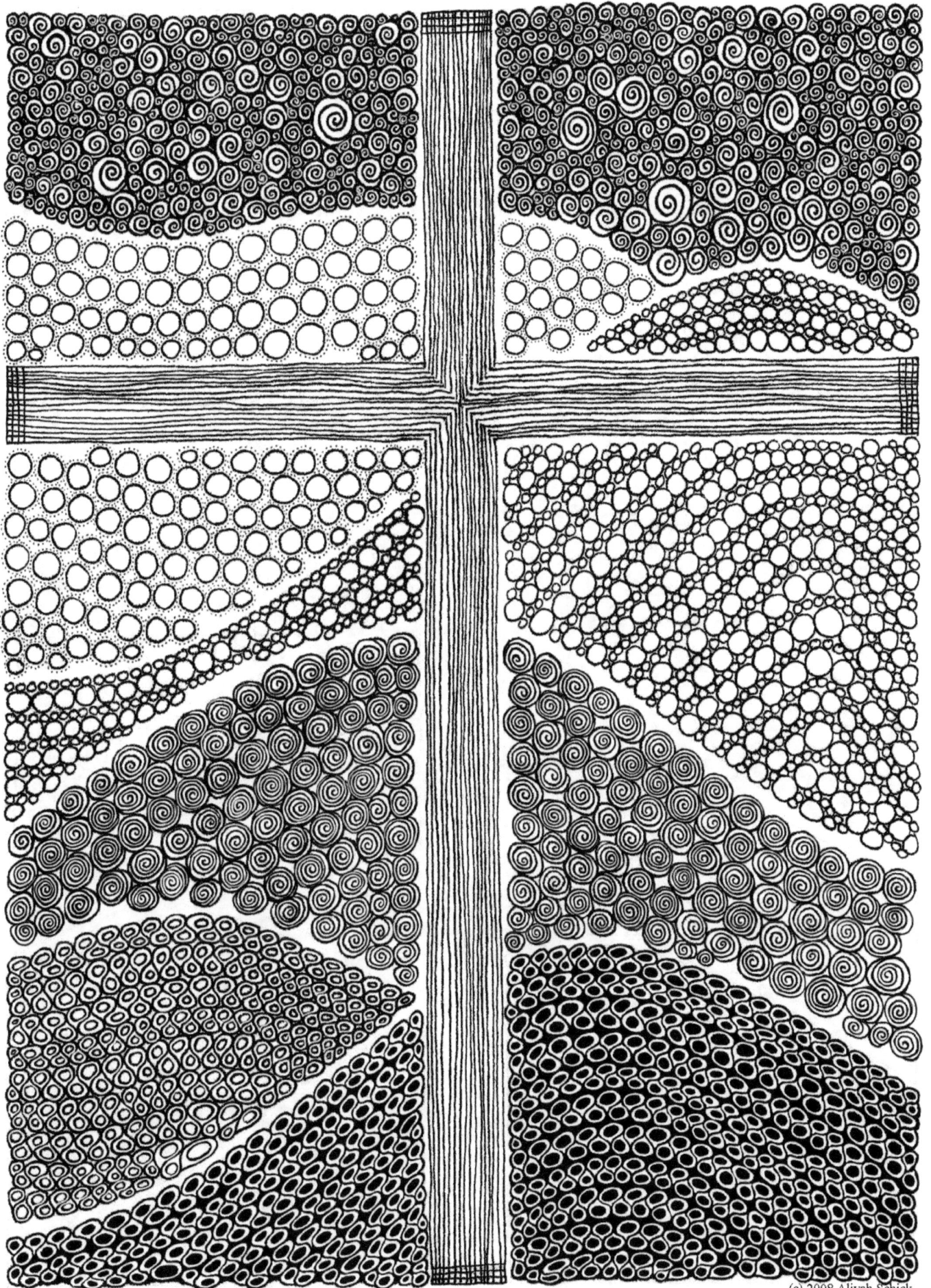

31

33

35

41

43

45

47

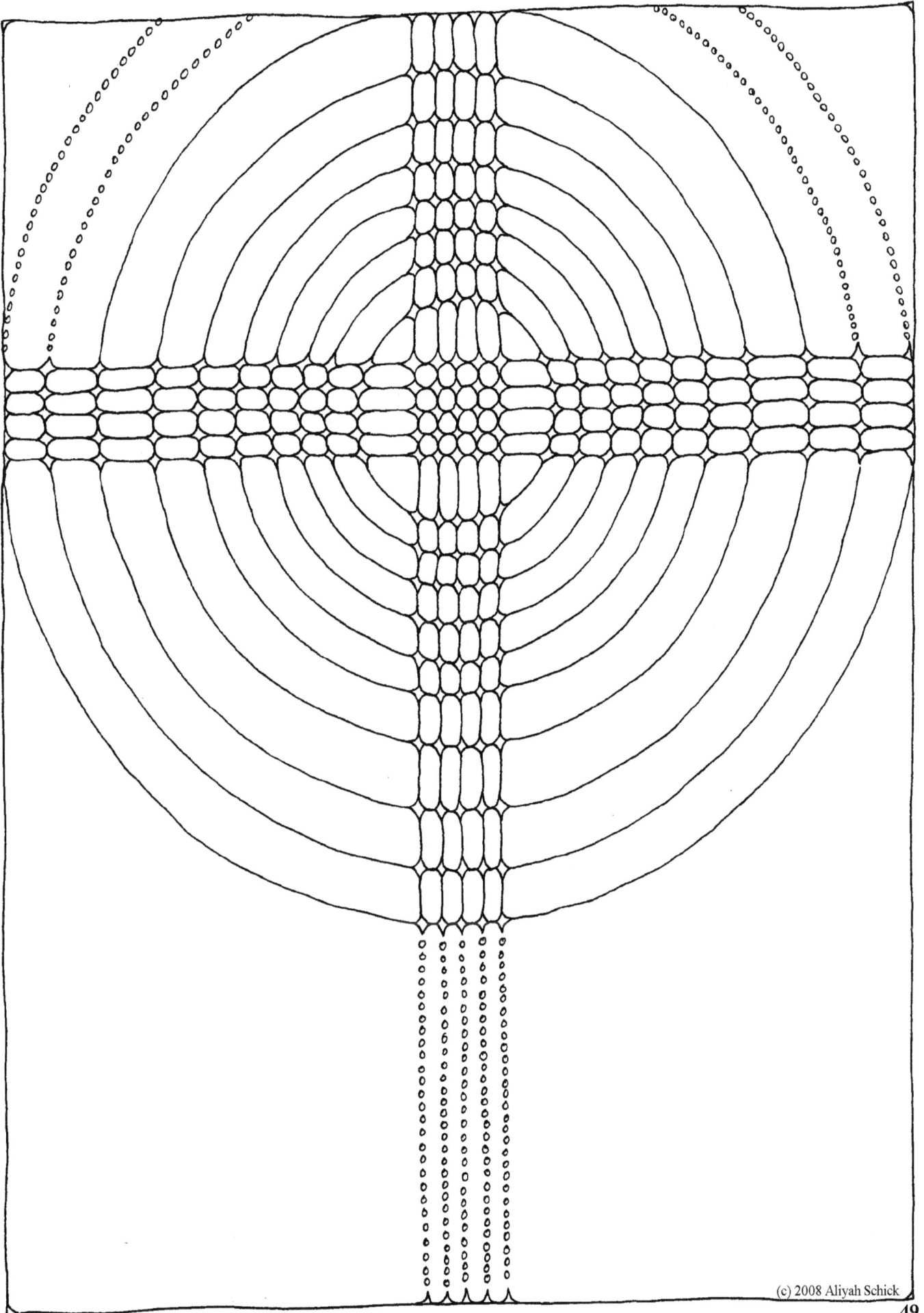

49

53

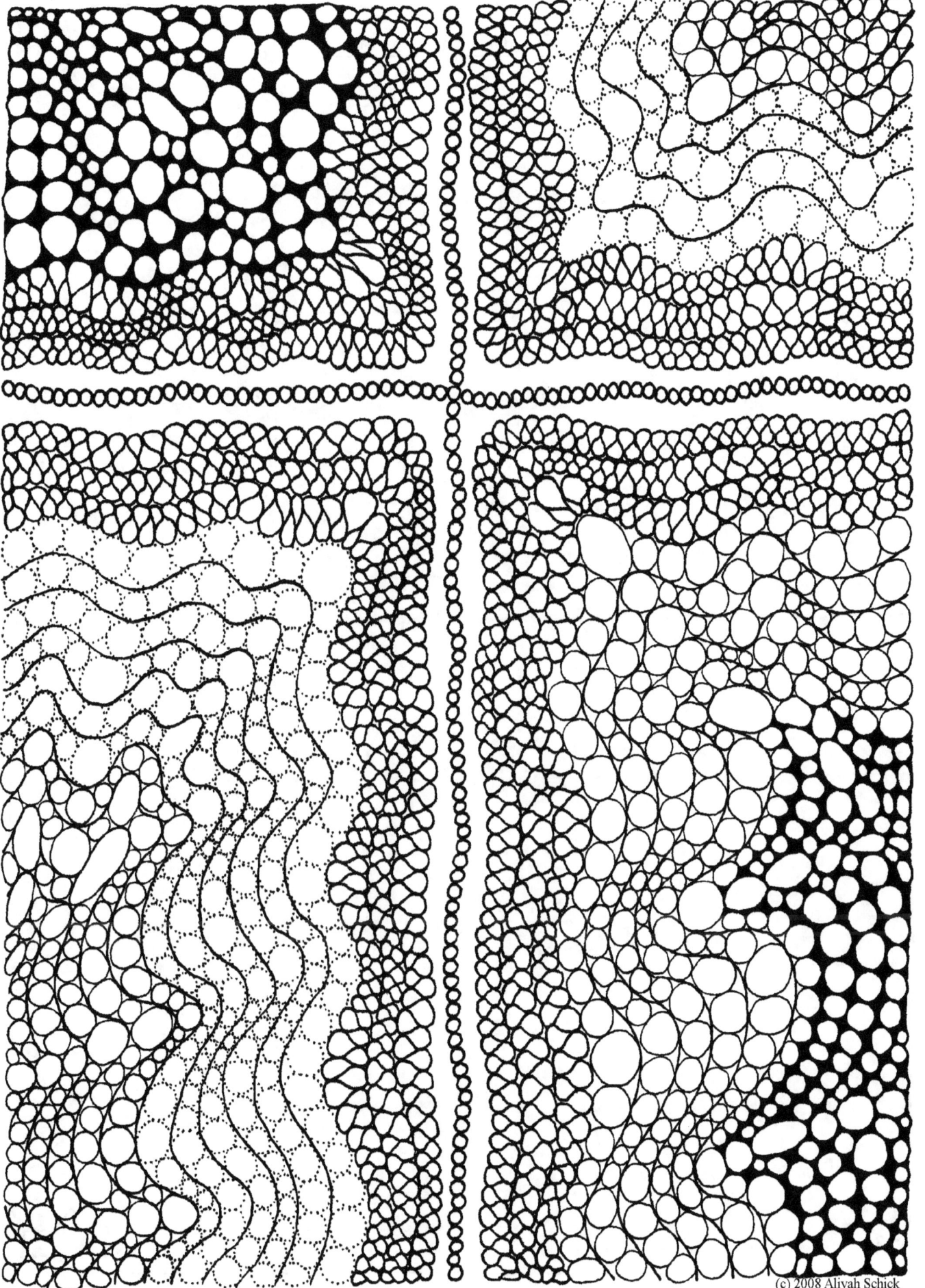

55

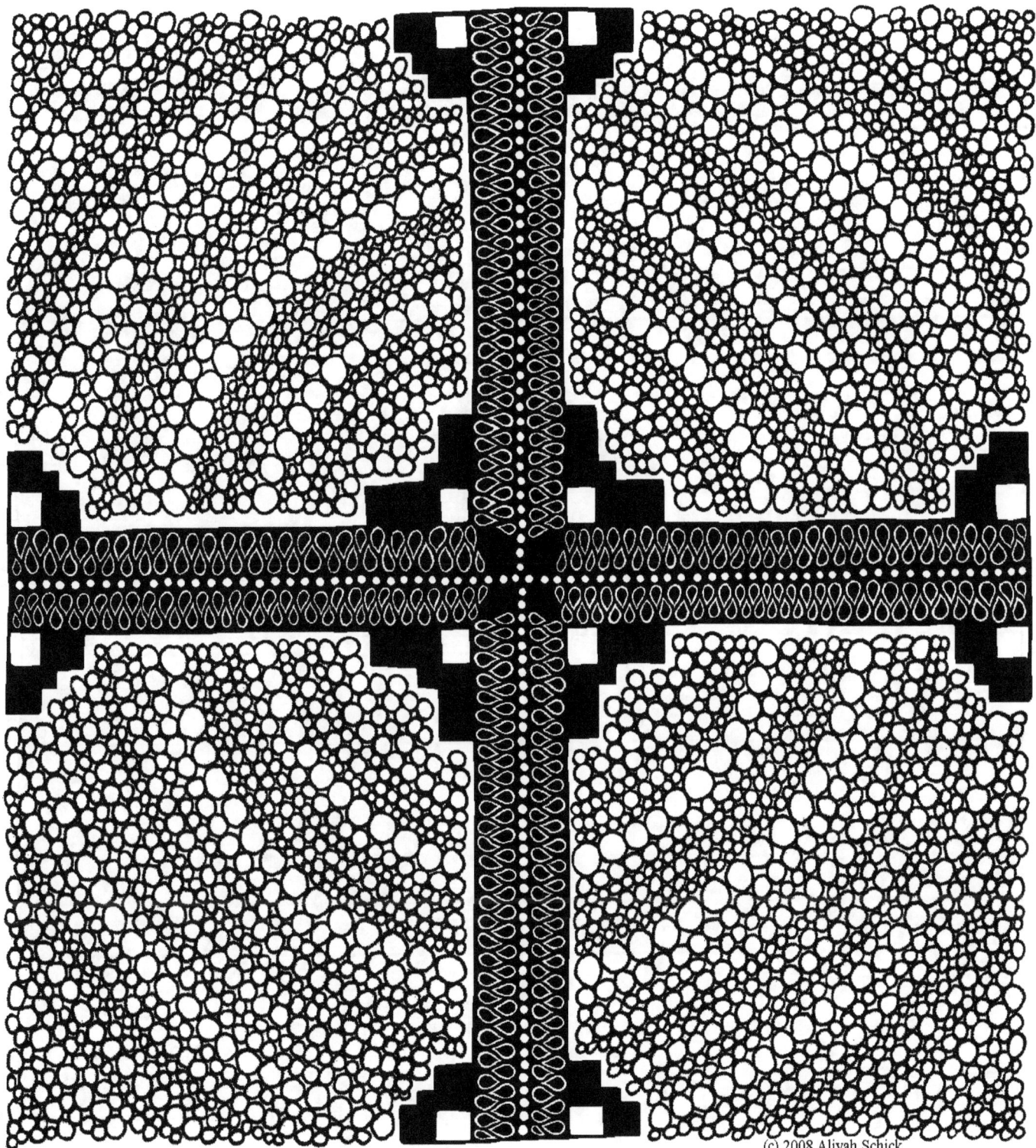

57

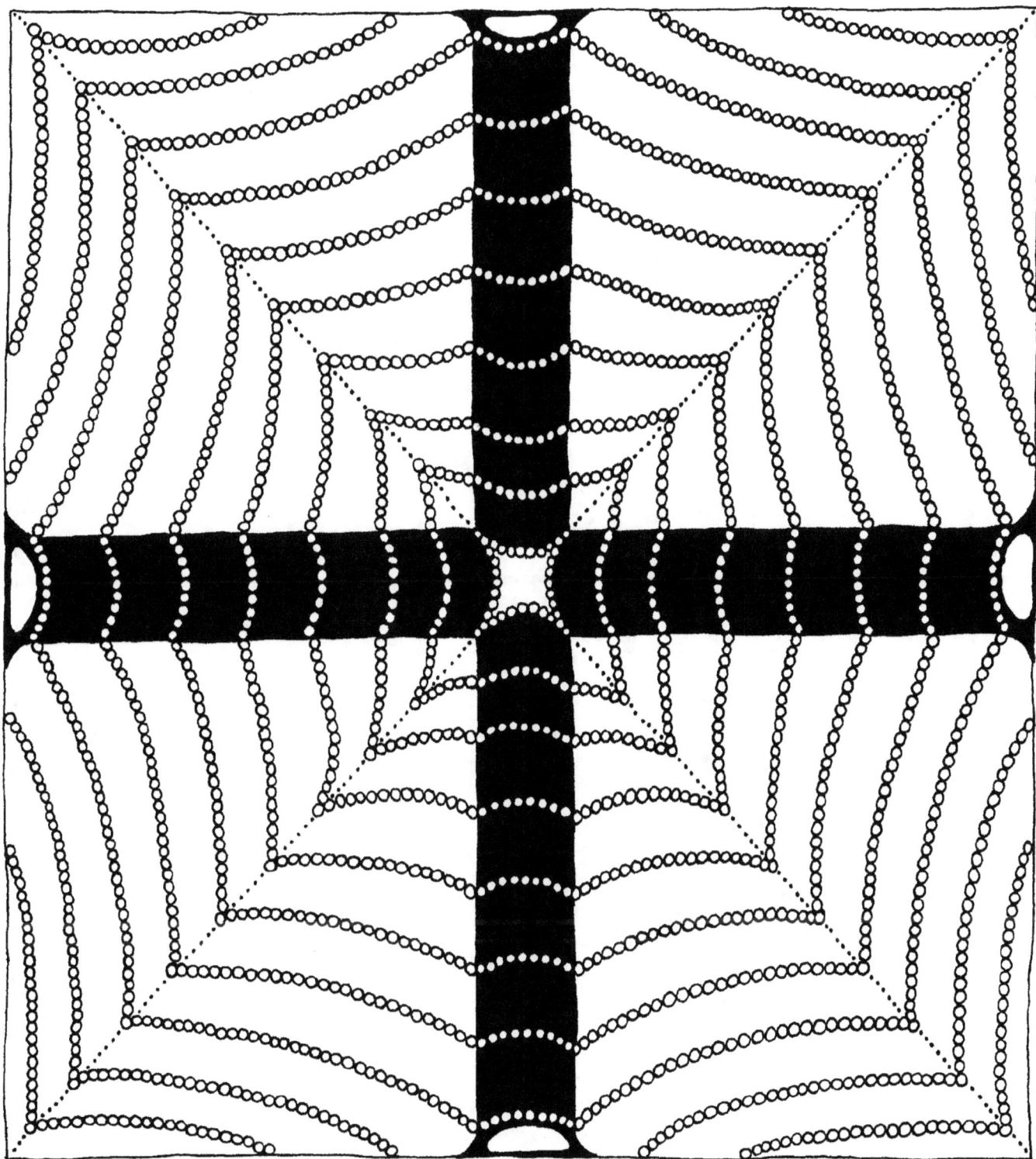

(c) 2008 Aliyah Schick

59

61

63

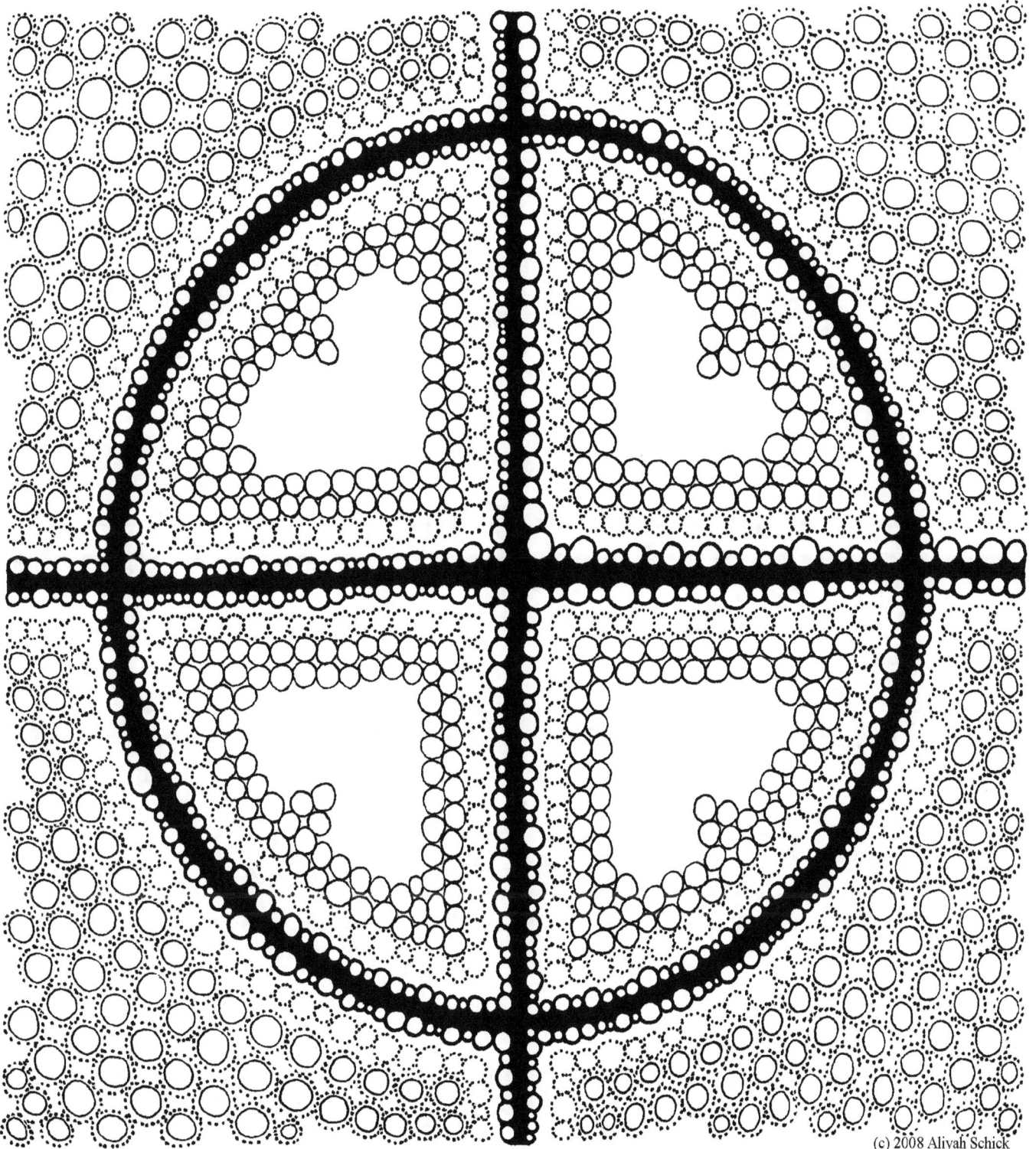

67

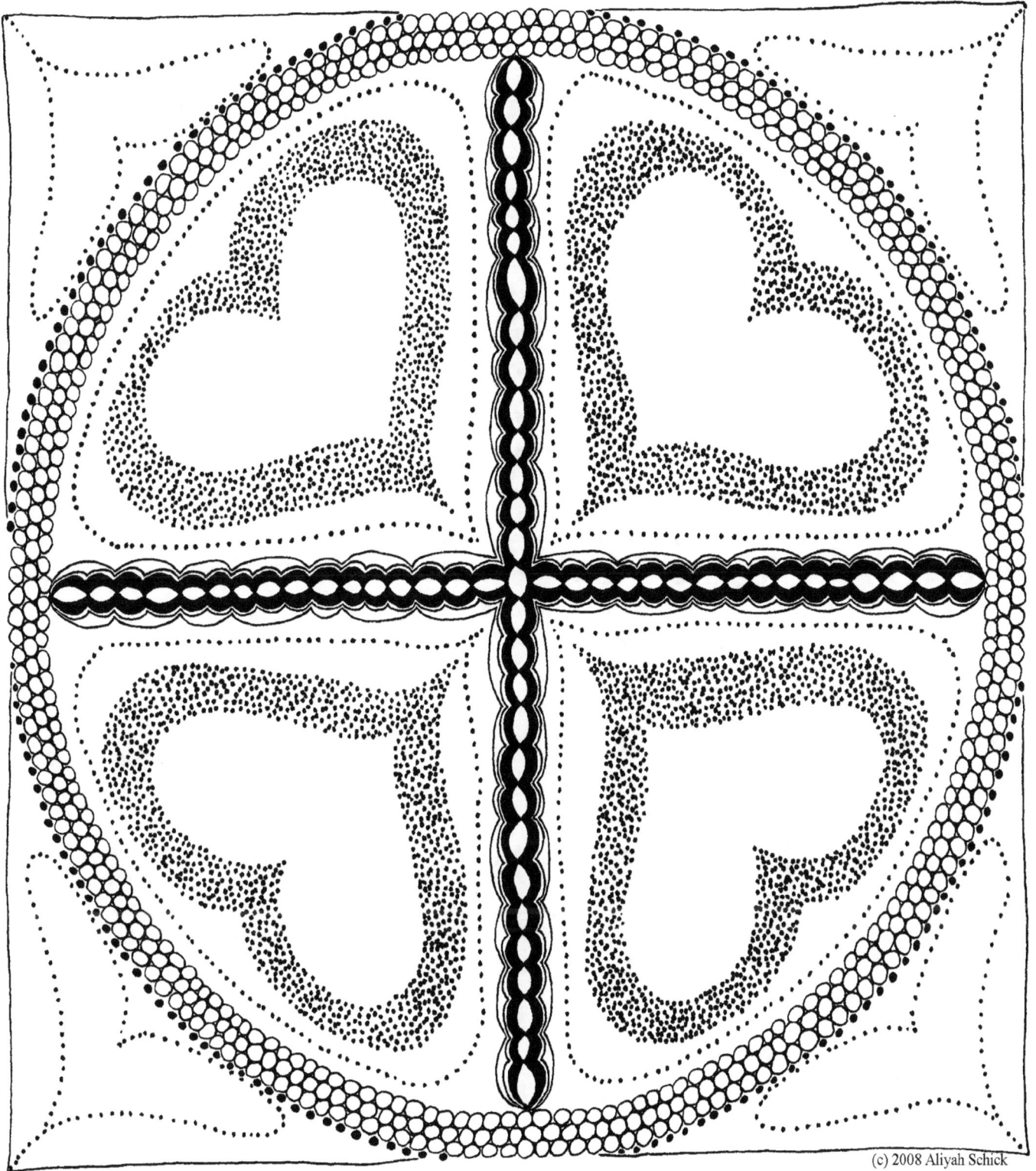

69

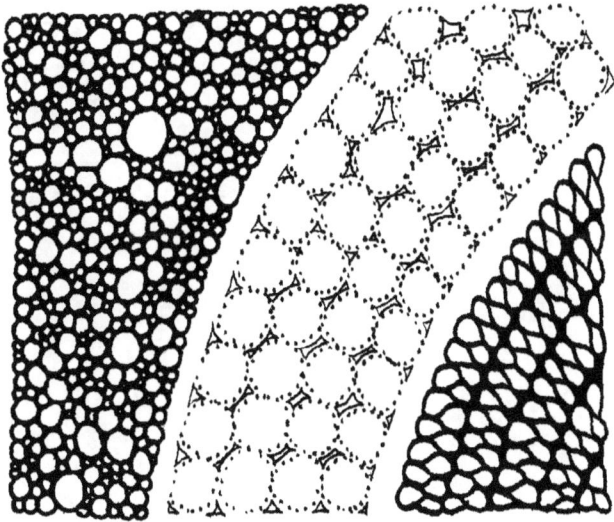
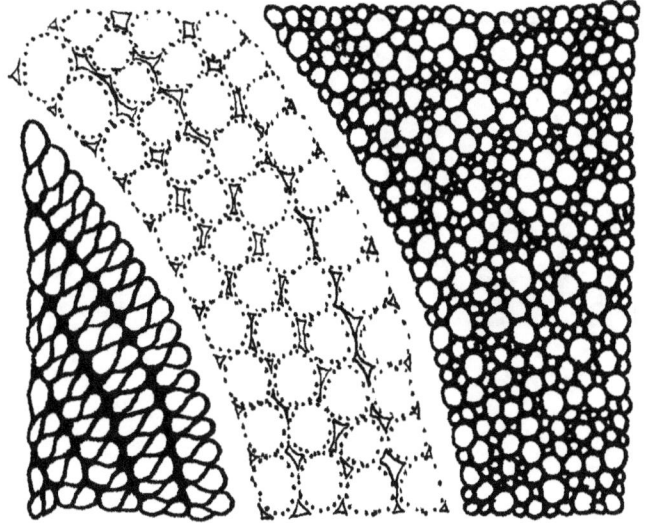
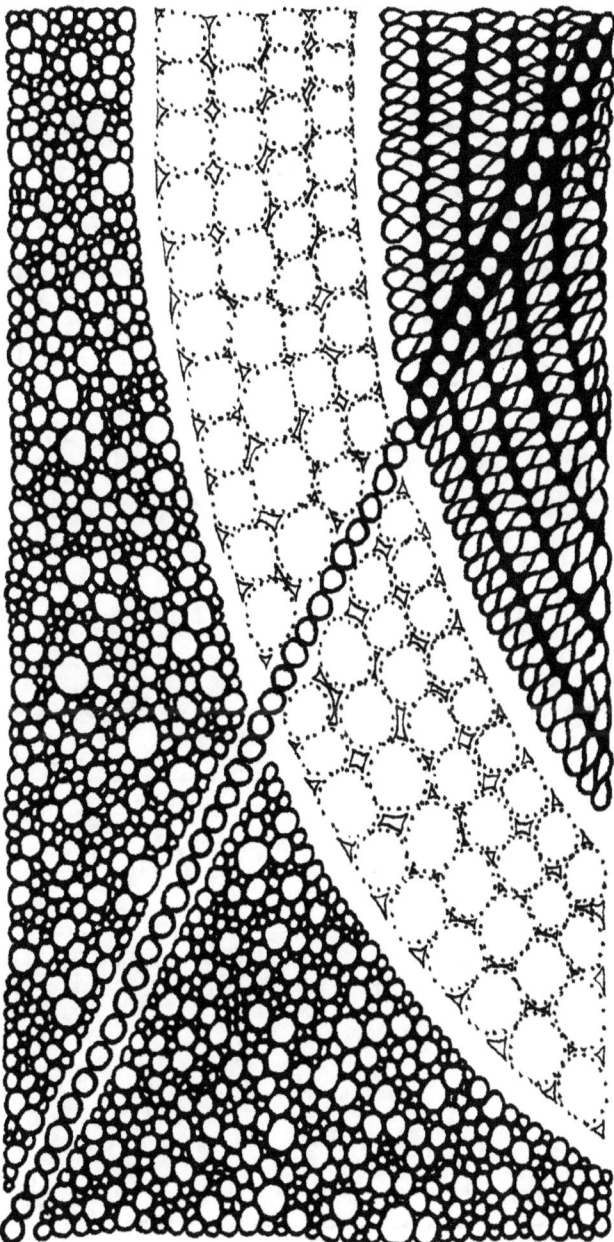
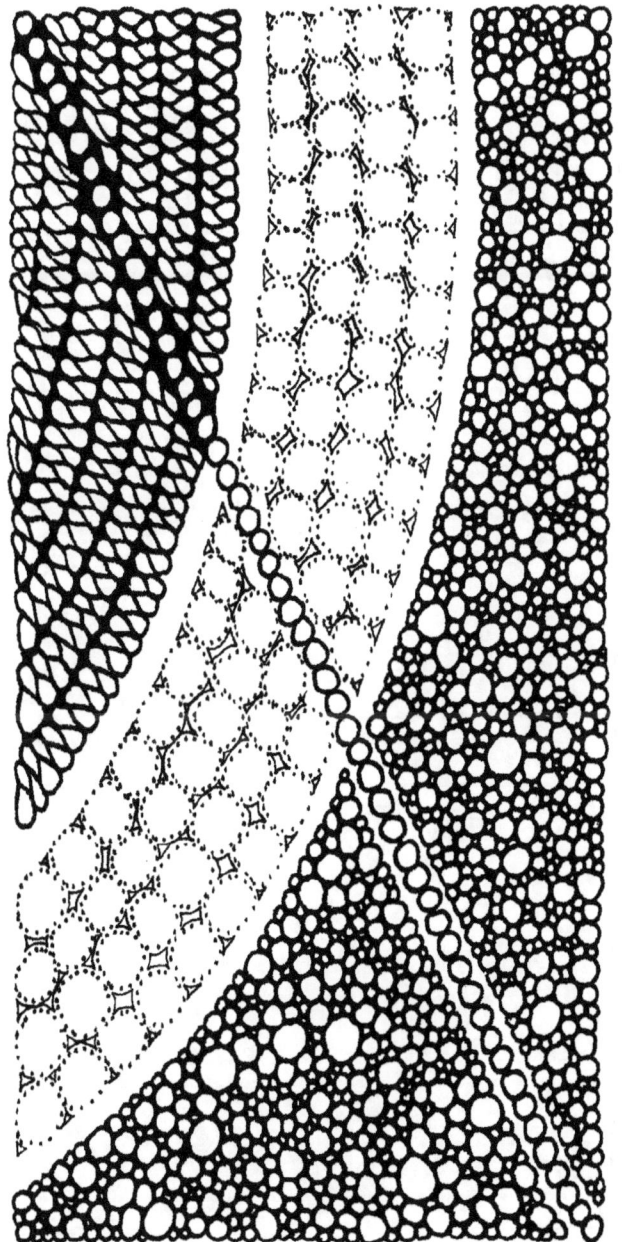

73

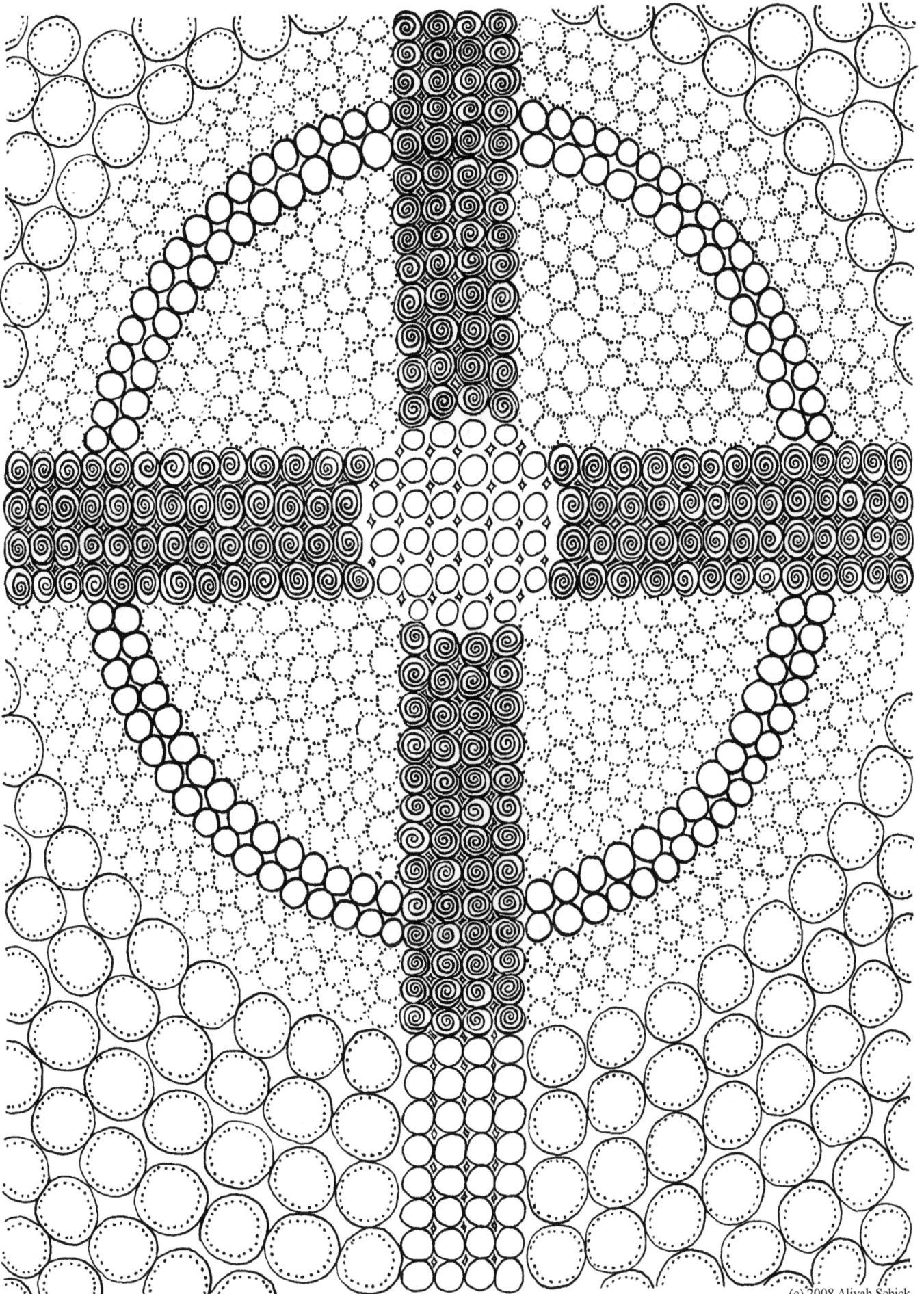

75

The Sacred Imprints™ Meditative Coloring Books
Five Volumes: Angels, Crosses, Ancient Symbols, Hearts, and Labyrinths

---

Meditative Coloring Book 1 -- Angels

The Sacred Imprints ™ Angelic images are drawn during a centering meditation. With a pen in each hand, Aliyah allows the lines to go where they will, the two sides mirroring each other. Every movement is guided by spirit; every drawing is different; and each one is a wonderful surprise filled with angelic presence.

Meditative Coloring Book 2 -- Crosses

The cross is one of our most ancient and enduring sacred symbols, found in nearly every culture throughout human existence. It symbolizes the celestial, spirtual divine coming into being in this material world. It represents God taking form, and the integration of soul into physical life. The drawings of the Crosses Series feature ancient and contemporary images of the cross in reflections of the deep spiritual significance of its form.

---

www.MeditativeColoring.com

Meditative Coloring Book 3 -- Ancient Symbols

Ancient and indigenous sacred images speak deeply to us, to our bellies and our bones, to our cellular memory and our wisdom, to our souls' yearnings. Native peoples throughout time and place see the sacred in all of life. For them, holiness is life and life is holiness. Life is the manifestation of the holy in all things. The drawings of the Ancient Symbols Series feature timeless designs used by every culture on earth to remind us of the sacred.

Meditative Coloring Book 4 -- Hearts

The heart is one of our favorite symbols, evoking feelings of love, caring, loyalty, and devotion. As you spend time with these Sacred Imprints Heart drawings, open your heart to live with more compassion for others and for yourself. Open your life to deeper connection with the earth and all of life. Open yourself to recognize the sacred in all things, including in yourself.

Meditative Coloring Book 5 -- Labyrinths

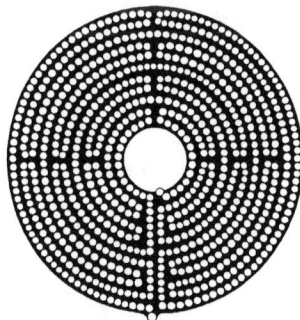

These original artist's labyrinth drawings invite you to color your steps into the labyrinth, one by one, as you contemplate, meditate, or pray. Go deep into your inner wisdom and guidance where questions' answers reveal themselves and choices come clear. Or simply relax and be with your breathing. Now you can bring your labyrinth with you to wherever you need to be.

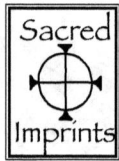

Sacred Imprints